CONTENTS

JUST WHAT YOU WANT

Are you a picky eater? Then you'll love Chipotle Mexican Grill®.

You get to control your food every step of the way. More onions? Less cheese? Skip the rice? No problem.

You can see all the ingredients spread out behind a glass shield. Your order travels down the line from worker to worker. At each stop, you choose exactly what you want.

FAVORITE FOOD FRANCHISES

CHIPOTLE

Laura Purdie Salas

Mitchell Lane
PUBLISHERS

Parent and Caregiver Tips for Creating Nonfiction Readers

The high-interest topics in the ***Favorite Food Franchises*** series are sure to get your young reader excited about reading nonfiction. While exploring a fascinating subject, your reader will be introduced to new facts, ideas, and vocabulary.

Tips for Reading Nonfiction

Talk about Nonfiction

Explain that nonfiction books provide facts about real-world topics. When readers read nonfiction, they gain a rich understanding of the world. They build background knowledge that provides a foundation for learning and academic success.

Look at the Parts

This book contains the following helpful features. Share the purpose of each feature with your reader.

Photos, Captions, and Graphic Aids
The photos, captions, maps, diagrams, time lines, and other graphic aids in nonfiction texts contain a wealth of information. Help your reader identify different ways information can be displayed.

Sidebars
These extra tidbits of information help satisfy readers' curiosity and expand their knowledge.

Table of Contents
Located at the front of the book, this list shows the big ideas within the text and the page numbers where they can be found.

Glossary
Located at the back of the book, the glossary defines key words and phrases that are related to the topic. These words and phrases can be found in the text in colored type.

Comprehension Questions (Fact Check)
Multiple-choice questions help readers self-check to make sure they understand what they read.

Index
Located at the back of the book, the index is an alphabetical list of topics and the page numbers where they can be found.

With a little help and guidance, your reader will be on their way to enjoying and learning from nonfiction books.

Mitchell Lane
PUBLISHERS
mitchelllanepub.com

2001 SW 31st Avenue
Hallandale, FL 33009

First Edition, 2025.
Author: Laura Purdie Salas
Designer: Rhea Magaro
Editor: Kim Thompson

Series: Favorite Food Franchises
Title: Chipotle Mexican Grill / by Laura Purdie Salas

Hallandale, FL : Mitchell Lane Publishers, [2025]

Library bound ISBN: 979-8-89260-311-9
Paperback ISBN: 979-8-89260-434-5
eBook ISBN: 979-8-89260-320-1

PHOTO CREDITS
Associated Press: JACK DEMPSEY, 11; Chipotle: cover, 1, 3, 4, 5, 6, 10, 13, 14, 18, 19, 20, 22, 24, 26, 28, 29; Beth Galton, 17; Kelly Lee, Mulberry Tree Design, 20; Media Wisdom Photography Ltd, 22; Shutterstock: dwph, cover; Eric Broder Van Dyke, 6; asad 0099, 7; rangizzz, 7, 8, 10, 13, 15, 17, 19, 23, 25, 27; NiglayNik, 8; Taras Vyshnya, 8; rblfmr, 15; The Image Party, 16; GagliardiPhotography, 16; Victor Moussa, 21; Triff, 22; Nolichuckyjake, 23; Jidev jidu photography, 23; Ljupco Smokovski, 27; IDEA ROUTE, 32

WHAT GOES INSIDE
CILANTRO-LIME RICE 130*
BLACK OR PINTO BEANS 120*
SALSA 15-80*
CHEESE OR SOUR CREAM 100-120*
GUACAMOLE (ADD 1.80) 150*
*Calorie Range
FEATURED ITEM
BURRITO BOWL
Naturally raised, tender carnitas with cilantro-lime rice, black beans, roasted chili-corn salsa and cheese.
6.35
620 Calories
EXTRAS
Chips & Guacamole 720* 2.95
Chips & Salsa 590-650* 1.65
Guacamole 150* 1.80
Chips 570* 1.15
*Calorie Range
ACT Natural

Chipotle is best known for its burritos. In the United States, a burrito is usually a flour **tortilla** stuffed with food. It might include rice, beans, meat, and vegetables. The tortilla is shaped into a tube and eaten with your hands.

The burritos at Chipotle are huge. Many weigh more than a pound. That's heavier than an entire loaf of bread or an NFL football.

Burrito Bites

Nobody's exactly sure how the burrito got its name. *Burrito* means "little donkey" in Spanish. One idea is that a burrito holds many fillings just like a donkey carries many things in its pack saddle.

Burrito Bites

Steve Ells has appeared on TV. He was a judge on a cooking competition show called *America's Next Great Restaurant*.

FANCY OR FAST?

Steve Ells is the **founder** of Chipotle. He attended **culinary** school and then became a chef at a famous restaurant called Stars. Stars was a fine-dining restaurant in San Francisco, California. When Ells worked there, he often ordered tacos and burritos from small casual restaurants in the neighborhood.

Ells dreamed of opening a **gourmet** restaurant of his own, but he didn't have enough money. He got the idea to start a fast-food restaurant to make money. Then, he could use his earnings to start the fancy restaurant he really wanted to run.

Ells knew nothing about starting a business. His family loaned him some money. He decided to try his luck in Colorado, where there were fewer Mexican restaurants.

Ells opened the first Chipotle near the University of Denver campus. The restaurant was small, just 850 square feet (79 square meters). It served its first customers in 1993.

Burrito Bites

A chipotle is a jalapeño pepper that has been smoked and usually dried.

Steve Ells

Chipotle was a hit. The fast, yummy, inexpensive food was popular with college students. Ells decided that because his new business was doing so well, the fine-dining restaurant of his dreams would have to wait.

THE CHIPOTLE WAY

Most Chipotle **franchises** have a similar look. They have concrete floors underfoot and exposed pipes overhead.

The furniture and the decorations use a lot of wood and steel. Many surfaces have hard edges. The design looks clean and basic. That's a good fit for a restaurant that focuses on basic ingredients.

Burrito Bites

Many Chipotles have wall sculptures made from wood and metal. They're inspired by the culture and gods of the Mayan people. Millions of people in southeastern Mexico and northern Central America are descendants of the Maya.

To place an order at Chipotle, you walk up to the counter. You follow your meal down the line as you give directions for adding every ingredient.

First, you choose tacos, a burrito, a bowl, or a salad. The next options are for rice and **proteins**. You select the beans and vegetables you want. Then, it's on to salsas and sauces, sour cream, and other toppings. Workers stuff, drip, drizzle, and arrange all your ingredients. The line ends at the cash register. You pay before carrying your **customized** meal to a table.

Burrito Bites

People love to share their favorite Chipotle creations. One TikTok video shows how to order ingredients and build a burrito for less money. More than 2.5 million people have watched it.

ALL ABOUT THE FOOD

There are many different kinds of burritos in Mexico and the U.S. One kind is the wet burrito. It's a stuffed tortilla that has sauce poured over it.

wet burrito

Another kind is the Mission burrito, which got its name from the Mission District of San Francisco. A Mission burrito includes rice in the filling. At restaurants that serve Mission burritos, customers often get to see the fillings on display and choose the ones they want. Ells loved those ideas. He based Chipotle's burritos on Mission burritos. He made them a lot bigger, though, and changed some of their traditional flavors.

Mission District of San Francisco, CA

Burrito Bites

Chipotle is so popular that many Americans define a burrito only by Chipotle's standards. That upsets some people. They want everyone to know about a wider variety of Mexican foods.

CHIPOTLE
for Real
CERTIFIED
ORGANIC
BLACK TEA

Chipotle's goal is to make real food from simple ingredients. Offerings contain only foods you can easily recognize. They don't have artificial flavorings or colors.

There are meats, beans, rice, cheese, grilled vegetables, guacamole, salsa, sour cream, and more. From these basic choices, there are countless combinations to try.

Chipotle's menu hasn't changed much over the years. One key addition was sofritas, a plant-based protein. Another popular add-on was queso blanco, a cheese sauce.

Burrito Bites

Chipotle has a secret menu of items that the restaurant can make, but that it doesn't advertise. The quesarito is the star of Chipotle's secret menu. It's a mammoth burrito wrapped inside a cheesy quesadilla.

Chipotle's chicken is **marinated** overnight in a spicy, smoky, peppery sauce. The next day, cooks grill it on the griddle.

Steak needs an extra cooking step. First, it's cooked **sous vide**. This long cook at a low temperature seals in moisture and flavor. Then, the steak is marinated. Finally, it gets grilled the next day.

Using fresh ingredients comes with risks. Raw foods that are not handled carefully can spread germs. In 2015, Chipotle was responsible for an outbreak of **E. coli** that made 52 customers sick. After that, the company focused on teaching workers how to keep food safe.

REAL SUCCESS

Steve Ells never started a fine-dining restaurant. Instead, he opened a second Chipotle location in 1995 and a third in 1996. By 2023, more than 3,000 Chipotle franchises were in operation.

Chipotles are spread across the United States. There are some locations in Canada and overseas. In 2023, the restaurant chain took in almost 10 billion dollars.

Hickory, NC

London, England

Burrito Bites

McDonald's invested in Chipotle in 1998. It owned about 90 percent of the company and helped it grow from 13 to more than 500 locations. In 2006, McDonald's sold its stake in Chipotle so it could focus on its own restaurants.

YOU'RE LOOKING AT THE COMPLETE LIST OF CHIPOTLE INGREDIENTS. FOR REAL.

Chipotle is proud of its commitment to real food. Its advertising reflects that.

One video is called "Back to the Start." It shows a farmer who uses new technology to produce more food. He realizes that more natural methods are better for people and the planet. Country music legend Willie Nelson provides the background music.

Another ad campaign was "As Real as It Gets." Comedians revealed their fears and secrets in each ad. This was supposed to highlight the way Chipotle keeps it real by not adding dyes, preservatives, or artificial flavors to its foods.

Burrito Bites

Even though Chipotle serves healthy food, customers must be aware of portion sizes. A burrito stuffed with rice, meat, and cheese can have over 1,000 calories.

CHIPOTLE Cultivate FOUNDATION

Chipotle runs the Cultivate Foundation. Its mission is to make real food available to everyone. The charity partners with groups that work to reduce food waste and encourage the fair treatment of animals.

Chipotle has come a long way since it was one little restaurant serving Mexican-inspired food. It's grown to be the second-largest Mexican restaurant chain in the United States. That's just keeping it real.

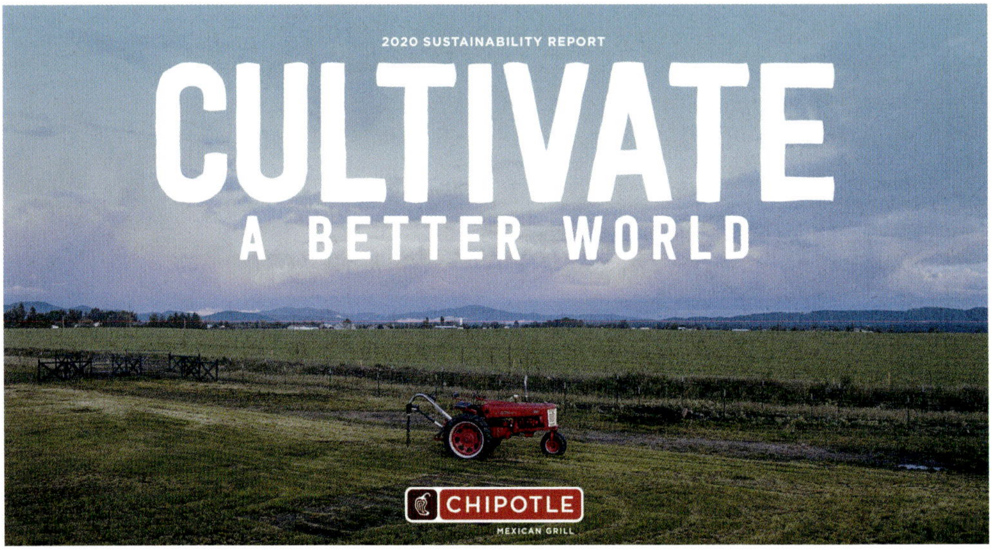

Burrito Bites

Many Chipotle locations participate in the company's Harvest Program. They donate their extra food to local food banks.

A CHIPOTLE TIME LINE

1993 Steve Ells opens the first Chipotle Mexican Grill in Denver, Colorado.

1996 Chipotle opens more Denver locations.

1998 McDonald's invests heavily in Chipotle.

1999 Chipotle spreads outside of Colorado.

2005 Salads appear on the Chipotle menu.

2014 A plant-based protein, sofritas, joins the menu.

2015 A string of illnesses is linked to food served at Chipotle.

2017 Steve Ells steps down from leading Chipotle.

2018 The former leader of Taco Bell becomes the head of Chipotle.

2023 Chipotle takes in almost 10 billion dollars.

Chipotle
BURRITOS & TACOS

GLOSSARY

culinary (KUH-luh-ner-ee)
of or relating to food and cooking

customized (KUHS-tuh-mized)
designed to suit someone's individual tastes and preferences

E. coli (ee-KOH-lie)
a type of bacteria that can breed in raw food and cause intestinal illness

founder (FOUN-dur)
the person who starts a company or organization

franchises (fran-CHYE-sis)
individual locations of a chain store or restaurant; legal agreements that let people run businesses that sell products created by a larger company

gourmet (goor-MAY)
of or relating to expensive or specialty food that requires expert preparation

marinated (MAR-i-nay-tid)
soaked in a sauce for added flavor and tenderness

proteins (PROH-teenz)
foods that have certain chemical compounds that are essential for life and that are found in meat, eggs, and other ingredients; usually but not always a kind of meat

sous vide (SOO-veed)
a cooking style that slowly cooks food sealed inside a pouch

tortilla (tor-TEE-uh)
a round, flat bread that is made from flour or cornmeal and that is often used in Mexican cooking

FACT CHECK

1. Chipotle customers can watch their food being _____.
   A. grilled B. prepared C. bought

2. Steve Ells started Chipotle so he could _____.
   A. afford to open a fine-dining restaurant
   B. learn to cook C. start a Mexican food empire

3. Chipotle is best known for its _____.
   A. burritos B. tacos C. beans

4. Steve Ells was inspired by food served in restaurants in _____.
   A. New York B. Denver C. San Francisco

Answers: 1. B, 2. A, 3. A, 4. C

FURTHER READING

Cohn, Jessica. *On the Job in a Restaurant*. South Egremont, MA: Red Chair Press, 2016.

Lowe, Lindsey. *Mexican Culture and Cooking*. New York: Cavendish Square, 2023.

Melian, Gaby. *Gaby's Latin American Kitchen: 70 Kid-Tested and Kid-Approved Recipes for Young Chefs*. Boston: America's Test Kitchen Kids, 2022.

ON THE INTERNET

Biz Kid$: Young Entrepreneur Profiles
https://bizkids.com/groups/profiles
Learn about young people who have started their own companies.

Food Network: Cooking with Kids
https://www.foodnetwork.com/recipes/packages/recipes-for-kids/cooking-with-kids
Find recipes from the network for fun in the kitchen.

Old El Paso: Kid-Friendly Mexican Recipes
https://www.oldelpaso.com/articles/kid-friendly-mexican-recipes
Learn to make something delicious.

INDEX

ABOUT THE AUTHOR

Laura Purdie Salas is an award-winning author who lives and writes in Minnesota. Her many books include poetry and nonfiction. Laura loves to read, play board games, knit, explore nature, and spend time with her husband and two daughters. She also eats way too much fast food! Laura's a picky eater who loves choosing her own ingredients. She enjoys Chipotle tacos with chicken, lettuce, just a bit of rice, fajita veggies, cheese, and hot salsa. Visit Laura at laurasalas.com.

FAVORITE FOOD FRANCHISES

CHIPOTLE MEXICAN GRILL

Does the thought of a warm tortilla wrapped around steak, beans, cheese, and sour cream make your mouth water? Then you're ready to learn about Chipotle Mexican Grill®, one of the biggest Mexican food chains in the United States. Discover how the company started in Denver, Colorado. Find out what item is only on the secret menu. Then, read the rest of the *Favorite Food Franchises* series for more fascinating facts.

ATOS 4.5

Chipotle Mexican Grill
ISBN 979-8-89260-434-5
90000 >
9 798892 604345

Mitchell Lane
PUBLISHERS
mitchellanepub.com